FunTime® Piano

Kids' Songs

Level 3A-3B

Easy Piano

This book belongs to: _____

Arranged by

Nancy and Randall Faber

Production Coordinator: Jon Ophoff
Design and Illustration: Terpstra Design, San Francisco
Engraving: Dovetree Productions, Inc.

FABER
PIANO ADVENTURES®
3042 Creek Drive
Ann Arbor, Michigan 48108

A NOTE TO TEACHERS

FunTime® Piano Kids' Songs is a collection of popular songs that bring special enjoyment to children. The sense of fantasy and humor of the selections will motivate and entertain the Level 3 piano student.

FunTime® Piano Kids' Songs is part of the *FunTime® Piano* series. "FunTime" designates Level 3 of the *PreTime® to BigTime® Piano Supplementary Library* arranged by Faber and Faber.

Following are the levels of the supplementary library, which lead from *PreTime®* to *BigTime®*.

PreTime® Piano	(Primer Level)
PlayTime® Piano	(Level 1)
ShowTime® Piano	(Level 2A)
ChordTime® Piano	(Level 2B)
FunTime® Piano	(Level 3A–3B)
BigTime® Piano	(Level 4)

Each level offers books in a variety of styles, making it possible for the teacher to offer stimulating material for every student. For a complimentary detailed listing, e-mail faber@pianoadventures.com or write us at the mailing address below.

Visit **www.PianoAdventures.com**.

Helpful Hints:

1. As rhythm is of prime importance, encourage the student to feel the rhythm in his or her body when playing popular music. This can be accomplished with the tapping of the toe or heel, and with clapping exercises.

2. Hands-alone practice is often helpful. Ensure that the playing is rhythmic even in hands-alone practice.

3. The songs can be assigned in any order. Selection is usually best made by the student, according to interest and enthusiasm.

ISBN 978-1-61677-628-2

TABLE OF CONTENTS

Be Our Guest

from Walt Disney's BEAUTY AND THE BEAST

Lyrics by HOWARD ASHMAN
Music by ALAN MENKEN

the dishes! They can sing! They can dance! Af - ter all, miss, this is

France! And a din - ner here is nev - er sec - ond best.

Go on, un - fold your men - u, take a glance, and then___

___ you'll be our guest! Oui, our guest! Be our guest!

Edelweiss

from *The Sound of Music*

Lyrics by OSCAR HAMMERSTEIN II
Music by RICHARD RODGERS

8

Yellow Submarine

from *YELLOW SUBMARINE*

Words and Music by
JOHN LENNON and PAUL McCARTNEY

10

We all live in a yel - low sub - ma - rine,

yel - low sub - ma - rine,

1.

yel - low sub - ma - rine.

2.

yel - low sub - ma - rine. And our friends_____ are all a -

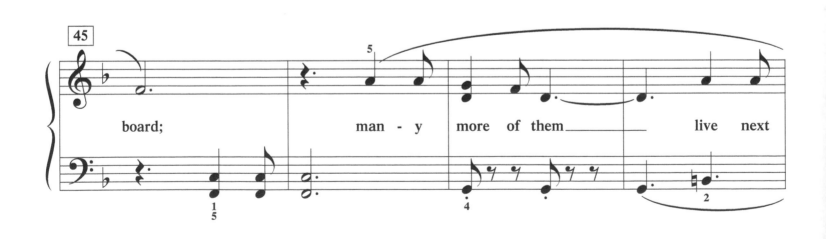

board; man - y more of them_____ live next

The Addams Family Theme

Theme from the TV Show and Movie

Music and Lyrics by
VIC MIZZY

Hello Muddah, Hello Fadduh!

(A Letter from Camp)

Words and Music by
ALLAN SHERMAN and LOU BUSCH

FF3004

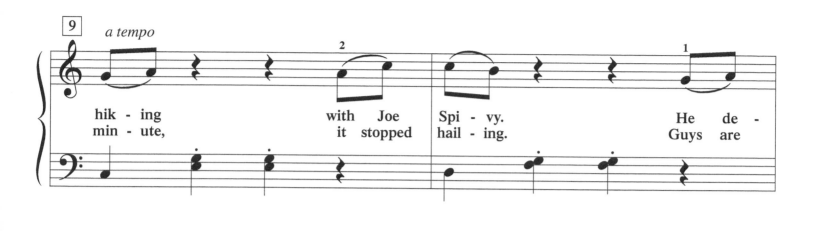

hik - ing / min - ute, with Joe / it stopped Spi - vy. / hail - ing. He de - / Guys are

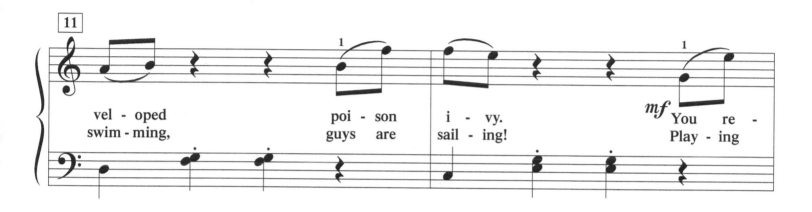

vel - oped / swim - ming, poi - son / guys are i - vy. / sail - ing! **mf** You re - / Play - ing

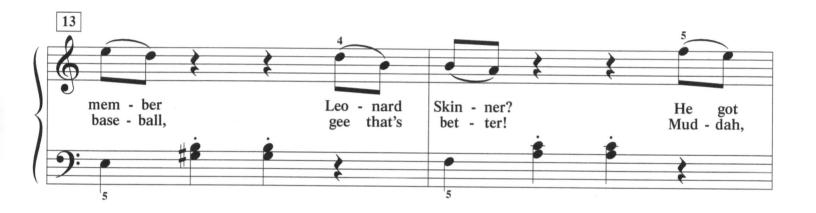

mem - ber / base - ball, Leo - nard / gee that's Skin - ner? / bet - ter! He got / Mud - dah,

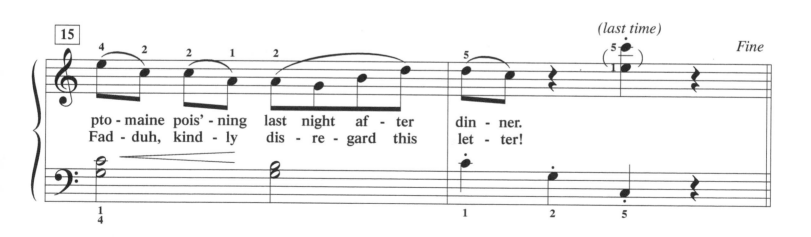

(last time)   *Fine*

pto - maine pois' - ning last night af - ter / din - ner.
Fad - duh, kind - ly dis - re - gard this / let - ter!

16

Arabian Nights

from Walt Disney's *ALADDIN*

Lyrics by HOWARD ASHMAN
Music by ALAN MENKEN

Walking on Sunshine

Words and Music by
KIMBERLEY REW

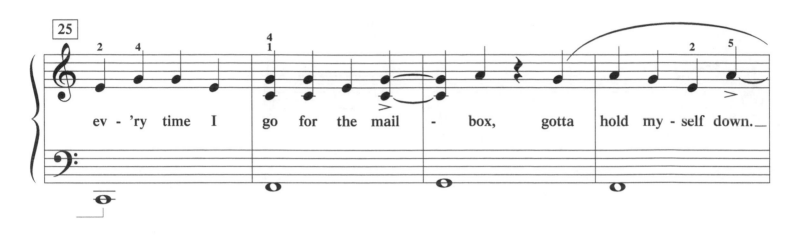

ev - 'ry time I go for the mail - box, gotta hold my - self down.___

'Cause

I just can't wait___ till you write___ me you're com - ing a - round.___

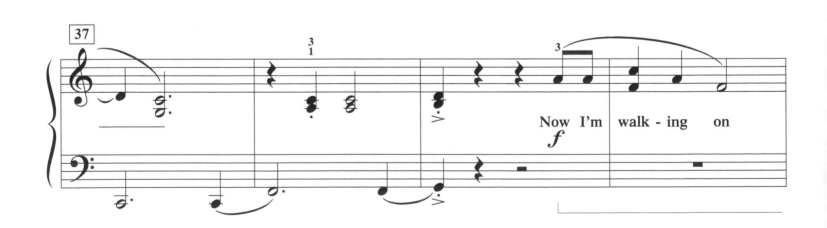

Now I'm walk - ing on

You've Got a Friend in Me

from Walt Disney's TOY STORY

Music and Lyrics by
RANDY NEWMAN

old   pal said.____   Son,   you've   got   a   friend   in   me.____

Yeah,   you've got a friend   in   me.   *mp*

mp Some oth-er folks   might be a   lit - tle bit smart-er than I   am,

You're gon - na see it's our des - ti - ny.

You've got a friend in me.

repeat!

You've got a friend in me.

Consider Yourself

from the Broadway Musical *OLIVER!*

Words and Music by
LIONEL BART

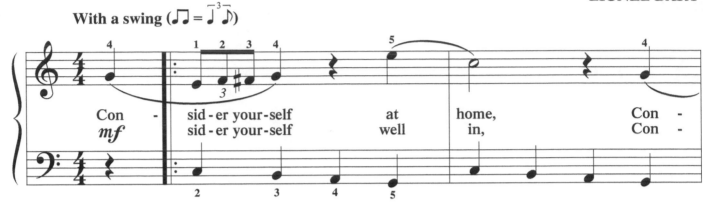

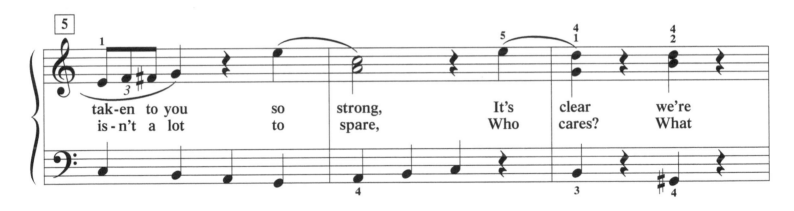

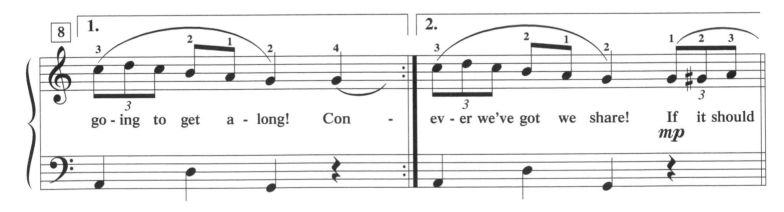

32

sid - er your - self   our   mate,   We

don't want to have   no   fuss,   For

af - ter some con - sid - er - a - tion,   we   can   state!   Con -

sid - er your - self   one   of   us!